AF399773

THE VIETNAM WAR

The Failure of Containment
in Southeast Asia

Written by Mylène Théliol
Translated by Rebecca Neal

THE VIETNAM WAR (1955-1975)

KEY INFORMATION

- **When:** 1 November 1955 to 30 April 1975.
- **Where:** Vietnam.
- **Context:** an ideological and military conflict between Communist North Vietnam (the Democratic Republic of Vietnam) and nationalist South Vietnam (the Republic of Vietnam), which was backed by the US armed forces, after the end of the First Indochina War (1946-1954).
- **Participants:** the Communist North Vietnamese army and the Viet Cong against the South Vietnamese and American armies.
- **Key protagonists:**
  - Ho Chi Minh (1890-1969), Vietnamese Communist leader and prime minister of the Democratic Republic of Vietnam (1945-1955), considered the father of North Vietnam.
  - Ngô Đình Diệm (1901-1963), Vietnamese anti-Communist politician and president of the Republic of Vietnam (1955-1963).

- Nguyên Van Thiêu (1923-2001), South Vietnamese army general and president of the Republic of Vietnam (1967-1975).
  - Lyndon B. Johnson (1908-1973), American politician and US president (1963-1969).
- **Death toll:**
  - Two million Vietnamese, including 1.3 million soldiers.
  - 60 000 American soldiers.

INTRODUCTION

The Vietnam War was one of the key events of the Cold War (1947-1991), as well as the longest and most destructive conflict in the history of US-Vietnamese relations.

After the First Indochina War against the French colonisers between 1946 and 1954, Vietnam was split into two territories, the Democratic Republic of Vietnam in the north and the Republic of Vietnam in the south. This division led to a military and political conflict which devastated the Vietnamese population during the 20 years of war that followed. When US forces entered the conflict in 1964, the discord between these two ideologically opposed populations only intensified, resulting in profound national trauma. Constant battles and bombing campaigns left the country drained and powerless to manage the vast quantities of toxic waste which continue to pose health risks to its inhabitants even today.

The Vietnam War had unprecedented consequences not only on American policy, but also on the American population, who witnessed the horrors of an all-out war against enemies who were sometimes impossible to detect or even figments of the US imagination. The conflict is etched into the memory of American veterans as a human disaster, and the damage inflicted on the Vietnamese population has yet to heal.

POLITICAL AND SOCIAL CONTEXT

FRENCH COLONIALISM IN INDOCHINA

Vietnam was a French colony from 1883 to 1954. It was made up of three states, Tonkin, Cochinchina and Annam, and from 1887 onwards was part of the Indochinese Union, which also comprised Laos and Cambodia. The country was partly run by the French colonisers, who developed an increasing number of tea, coffee, rice, pepper and rubber plantations and mined coal, zinc and tin for the profit of mainland France. The country's indigenous inhabitants did not have the same rights as its European minority: even though the *Code de l'indigénat* ("Code of the Indigenate") and the system of forced acculturation were not applied, unlike in France's African colonies, the native Vietnamese formed a diverse proletariat who worked in the country's rice fields, factories and mines.

THE *CODE DE L'INDIGÉNAT*

The *Code de l'indigénat* was a piece of legislation introduced in French colonies in 1887. It divided the population into two categories: French citizens from France and French subjects (Africans, Algerians, Malagasy, Antilleans, and so on), who were deprived of most of their freedoms and political rights. Their civil rights were limited to the right to follow their religion and traditional customs. The code's discriminatory measures included forced labour, the requisitioning of indigenous inhabitants' property and head taxes on the reservations, among others.

Acculturation in the colonies was based on assimilation or coexistence: indigenous inhabitants were forced to learn about the colonisers' culture through secular and religious schools, and their traditions were denigrated in favour of Western customs. The colonial administration rejected traditional thinking and ways of life, and imposed a system and lifestyle modelled on those of Europe.

The native Vietnamese faced difficult working conditions, and corporal punishment and pay deductions were common occurrences. The mistreatment of workers created a breeding ground for nationalist and Communist movements such as the Communist Party of Vietnam (CPV), which was founded in 1930 by Nguyễn Sinh Cung (1890-1969), who later assumed the name Ho Chi Minh.

| Ho Chi Minh in 1921.

The CPV was initially part of the French Communist Party, but in May 1931 joined the Communist International and adopted the name Indochinese Communist Party (ICP). The ICP was responsible for the first calls for independence, which became more vociferous in 1941 when Ho Chi Minh founded the Viet Minh, which brought together the ICP and several nationalist groups. The Viet Minh paved the way for anti-French and then anti-Japanese resistance, as Indochina was occupied by Japanese forces between March and September 1945.

The movement became particularly active from early 1945 onwards thanks to material support from the USA, which had decided to drive the French out of Indochina following the Yalta Conference (4-11 February 1945) and the Potsdam Conference (17 July-2 August 1945). However, after the fall of the Vichy regime and the liberation of France, the country's new provisional government, led by General Charles de Gaulle (1890-1970), directed new efforts at its colony in Indochina, and British and Japanese troops left the territory.

However, the Viet Minh and other independence movements were trying to gain control of Vietnam, and Ho Chi Minh called for a general insurrection on 13 and 19 August 1945. His party subsequently took control of all Hanoi's public services, and by 20 August, Tonkin (North Vietnam) was entirely controlled by revolutionary committees.

In response to attacks on French citizens, France sent armed troops to the region. Negotiations with the Viet Minh led to the signature of the Ho-Sainteny agreement on 6 March 1946, in which France recognised Vietnam as a free, but not independent, state. However, France proved unwilling to respect its colony's new status, and decided to reopen hostilities and take control of the territory by force. This resulted in open war between France and Vietnam.

THE FIRST INDOCHINA WAR (1946-1954)

After Japanese troops withdrew from Indochina, France wanted to regain control of its Asian colonies, particularly Vietnam. At that time, the country was controlled by the Viet Minh, who wanted to turn it into an independent Communist republic.

The war began on 23 November 1946 with the bombing of the major industrial city of Haiphong, which was taken back from the Communists after a series of destructive raids. The Viet Minh retaliated by executing French soldiers in Hanoi on 19 December. As a result, the simmering tensions between Ho Chi Minh's Viet Minh and the French colonial troops, who wanted to preserve mainland France's grip on Vietnam, developed into a full-blown war that would last for eight years.

Although the French army was modern and disciplined, it proved unable to counter the surprise attacks and guerrilla tactics favoured by the Vietnamese. Before long, the fighting intensified and other countries entered the conflict. China, which was now a Communist nation following the victory of Mao Zedong's (1893-1976) forces in its civil war, provided military support to the Viet Minh forces, while the USA began backing France in 1950, around the time of the outbreak of the Korean War (1950-1953). In particular,

American aerial support allowed France to regain the upper hand on the ground until 1951, after which a change of command in the French Far East Expeditionary Corps and the condemnation of the conflict by numerous French socialist and Communist intellectuals, who saw it as too costly and morally unjustifiable, slowed the French momentum.

France's plan was to concentrate the Viet Minh in a single location. To this end, Operation Castor aimed to capture Điện Biên Phủ, a city situated in a basin near the borders with Laos and China which allowed for both aerial and ground manoeuvres. The French army aimed to corner the Vietnamese forces, but ended up closing in on itself so that it was the colonial army that was trapped. Fighting lasted from March to 7 May 1954, when the French troops surrendered, signalling the resounding failure of the Điện Biên Phủ offensive. The French government then began negotiations, and a peace treaty was signed in Geneva on 20 and 21 July 1954. The terms of this agreement included the independence of Laos and Cambodia and the partition of Vietnam.

The Battle of Điện Biên Phủ put an end to French involvement in Indochina and led to the Geneva Accords, which partitioned Vietnam into two separate nations to the north and south of the 17th parallel, made provisions for elections to be held in all the states of Indochina by July 1956, stipulated the withdrawal of all French troops from the country within 300 days, and obliged the Viet Minh to leave Laos and Cambodia. The inhabitants of Vietnam then had to choose between the north and the south.

As a result of this partition, North Vietnam became a democratic socialist republic headed by the new president Ho Chi Minh, who wanted to unify the country under his leadership. To this end, he sought to recommence armed struggle in order to bring South Vietnam under his control and rescue the 10 000 to 15 000 Communist Party members living there.

South Vietnam enjoyed the economic and military backing of the USA, and was led by Ngô Đình Diệm, who established a nationalist, anti-Communist dictatorship in 1956. This constituted a rejection of the Geneva Accords, which stipulated that free elections were to be held in the country.

Opposition soon emerged to Diệm's imperialistic, pro-American policy. This included groups such as the National Liberation Front of South Vietnam, which was founded in December 1960, was led by Nguyễn Hữu Thọ, and comprised a mixture of Catholics, Buddhists and Communists. It had its own army, made up primarily of soldiers from both halves of the country and peasants who had been trained to fight. The group was called the Viet Cong by its enemies, namely the South Vietnamese regular army and the American troops, and this is the name under which it is best-known in the English-speaking world today.

In 1955, the Viet Cong decided to overthrow Diệm, and was supported by North Vietnam, Mao's Communist China, and the USSR. As a result of the system of alliances with the USA, the clash between the Viet Cong and Diệm's troops led to the outbreak of a simmering, nameless conflict that later became known as the Vietnam War. The war lasted for 20 years and resulted in the reunification of Vietnam in 1975, but its consequences were disastrous for the country.

KEY PROTAGONISTS

HO CHI MINH

| Photograph of Ho Chi Minh, taken in around 1946.

Nguyễn Sinh Cung, as he was originally known, was born in French Indochina to a father who was a Confucian scholar and grew up in a culturally rich environment, attending both French and Annamite schools. In accordance with Confucian tradition, at the age of ten he was given a new name, Nguyễn Tất Thành ("Nguyễn the Accomplished"). He was open to reformist ideas, which suggested that conditions in Indochina could gradually improve under French leadership, and began to reflect on the political situation in his country.

As a sailor, he travelled around the world, before moving to Paris in 1919 and becoming part of a network of intellectuals who reflected on the question of colonialism. It is at this point that he began to be influenced by Communist thought. He contributed to a journal, *Le Paria* ("The Pariah"), which advocated on behalf of colonised populations, and began using the name Nguyễn Ái Quốc ("Nguyễn the Patriot").

In 1923, he left France for Moscow and, having been won over by Marxism-Leninism, worked for the Third International, where he received his first political training. As part of a mission for the Comintern in Canton in 1925, he founded a school which trained young Vietnamese revolutionaries and prepared them to operate in organised cells in their homeland. Under threat of arrest, he fled to Hong Kong, where he founded the Vietnamese Communist Party in 1930. It was renamed the Indochinese Communist Party (ICP) the following year.

From 1933 to 1938, he worked in Moscow but lost his position with the Comintern, although he emerged unscathed from Stalin's Great Purge. He subsequently travelled to China, before returning to Indochina in 1941. He settled in the north of the country, where he lived in a cave and endured difficult conditions as a member of the underground resistance. As the influence of Communism in Vietnam continued to grow, he began to write more and founded the Viet Minh in collaboration with assorted nationalist groups. It was at this time that he adopted the name Ho Chi Minh, which means "Ho who has been enlightened".

After trying to establish contact with American forces in China, he was imprisoned and transferred from prison to prison for a period of two years. Once he was released, he got in touch with the American army, who supported him in anti-Japanese resistance activities.

In August 1945, when Japan surrendered, the Viet Minh seized power in Vietnam. On 2 September, Ho Chi Minh proclaimed the country's independence in front of an enthusiastic crowd in Hanoi.

However, this euphoria was short-lived: the Viet Minh only controlled half the country, and France wanted to regain its hold over its former colony. This led to the First Indochina War, which ravaged the country from 1946 to 1954. The Geneva Conference put an end to the conflict and resulted in partial victory for the Communists: while Ho Chi Minh was now recognised as the leader of the Democratic Republic of Vietnam in the north of the country, Vietnam was divided into two separate nations, with an anti-Communist regime governing the south.

When Ho Chi Minh died on 2 September 1969, the Second Indochina War (better known as the Vietnam War) between the Soviet- and Chinese-backed North Vietnam and the US-supported South Vietnam was well underway. It did not end until six years after his death, and resulted in the reunification of the country.

After his death, Ho Chi Minh was venerated by Vietnamese Communists, who considered him to be the father of the nation. His body was displayed in an opulent mausoleum in Hanoi, and the former capital of South Vietnam, Saigon, was renamed Ho Chi Minh City in homage to him.

NGÔ ĐÌNH DIỆM

| Ngô Đình Diệm in 1957.

Ngô Đình Diệm was the son of a Catholic mandarin (a government official under the Chinese

Empire), and also served as a mandarin under the emperor Bảo Đại (1913-1997) during the interwar period, before being appointed interior minister in 1933. He headed a commission tasked with reforming the country, but was left frustrated when France rejected his proposals for legislative reforms and resigned after three months. He even accused the emperor of being an instrument of French colonial policy.

He was a staunch anti-Communist and opted to go into self-imposed exile in the USA in 1945 rather than join Ho Chi Minh's new Communist government in the Democratic Republic of Vietnam. However, shortly after the Geneva Conference in 1954, Bảo Đại summoned him to form a new government in South Vietnam.

Initially, Diệm seemed to respect the Geneva Accords and organised a referendum. However, the vote was rigged and served as a pretext to overthrow the emperor and seize power for himself. He then founded the Republic of Vietnam, established an authoritarian regime and ruled the country alongside his family, whom he appointed to positions of power. He wanted this new nation to be a Catholic country, and therefore rejected Chinese culture, Buddhism and Communism.

His reforms met with fierce opposition within the country, and Buddhist and Communist parties joined forces to form the National Liberation Front of South Vietnam. His own generals also tried to overthrow him and install a new leader on several occasions, but the president enjoyed the support of the USA, who saw him as a serious rival to Ho Chi Minh. This understanding allowed the two countries to halt the spread of Communism in Vietnam, in line with the USA's policy of containment as set out by the Truman Doctrine in 1947.

Diệm's unpopularity was starkly illustrated by the Buddhist revolt and the self-immolation of the Buddhist monk Thích Quảng Đức (1893-1963) in June 1963 in protest at the government's repression of Buddhists.

| The self-immolation of Thích Quảng Đức, June 1963.

Tensions mounted throughout the summer of 1963, and in the end the president's generals decided to make another attempt to depose him. The rebellion was organised by the CIA and carried out by General Dương Văn Minh (1916-2001) on 2 November 1963, resulting in the execution of Diệm and his brothers. After a second coup d'état in 1965, Nguyễn Văn Thiệu assumed power in South Vietnam.

NGUYỄN VĂN THIỆU

| Nguyễn Văn Thiệu in 1967.

Nguyễn Văn Thiệu was the son of a landowner and studied in Saigon and France, before working on his family's farm during the Second World War. After 1945, he joined the nationalist and Communist forces of the Viet Minh under Ho Chi Minh. However, he soon came to view the acts of violence committed by the Communists as intolerable and attended the French Merchant Marine Academy between 1946 and 1947, before enrolling at the military army in Huế on 1 October 1948.

He joined the Vietnamese National Army in June 1949 in order to fight against the Viet Minh during the First Indochina War. He was successively promoted to lieutenant (1949), captain (1952) and commander of the 11th infantry division (1953).

After the Geneva Conference and the creation of the Republic of South Vietnam, Thiệu continued his military training at the military academy of Dalat, formerly the military academy of Huế. After being promoted to the rank of colonel in 1959, he left to study at the Fort Bliss military base in Texas for two years. He converted to Catholicism in 1960.

On his return to South Vietnam, he commanded various infantry divisions between 1961 and 1962.

On 2 November 1963, he took part in the coup d'état which overthrew Ngô Đình Diệm, and he held positions in the successive governments which ruled Vietnam over the following two years. On 19 and 20 February 1965, Vietnam's generals launched another coup which deposed the general Nguyễn Khánh (1927-2013), who had led South Vietnam since 1964.

After this revolt, Thiệu found himself at the head of the country's ruling military junta. He became president in 1967, in the middle of the Vietnam War. He centralised power in his own hands, limited the authority of the National Assembly and implemented agrarian reforms in order to improve living conditions for farmers and increase rice yields. He depended on US support, and assisted the Americans in their fight against the Viet Cong in order to weed out Communism in South Vietnam.

He was re-elected in 1971, and in 1973 he signed the Paris Peace Accords which made provisions for the progressive withdrawal of American troops from Vietnam. The last American sol-diers left the country in 1975, leaving the South Vietnamese army to grapple with the Viet Cong and the Communist North Vietnamese army.

It did not take long for the Communists to conquer all of Vietnam, forcing the desperate inhabitants of South Vietnam to flee to Europe and the USA. Thiệu was left with no choice but to resign on 21 April 1975, and lived in exile in the USA for the rest of his life.

LYNDON B. JOHNSON

| Lyndon B. Johnson in 1969.

Lyndon B. Johnson was the son of a Congressman from Texas, and always seemed destined to follow in his father's footsteps. He initially worked as a teacher, but soon resigned to focus his attentions on politics. From 1935 to 1937, he headed the Texas National Youth Administration, and in 1937 he was elected Congressman. He served in the House, representing the Democratic Party, until 1949, when he was elected senator, remaining in the Senate until 1961. He then grew close to the new president, John F. Kennedy (1917-1963), who was elected in 1960.

He served as vice-president under Kennedy and was sworn in as president on 22 November 1963, shortly after the latter's assassination. Almost a year later, he defeated the Republican Barry Goldwater to be elected in his own right.

During Johnson's presidency, the USA entered the war directly alongside the South Vietnamese armed forces against the Communist insurgents. The new president also took steps to combat racial discrimination and introduced his Great Society programme, which provided environmental protection, support for education, urban renewal, crime prevention measures, improvements in the healthcare system, and civil rights legislation to help black Americans.

However, the Vietnam War was a source of great tension in America and was proving increasingly costly: the USA spent $20 billion on the war in 1967, compared with $103 million in 1965. 1968 was a disastrous year for Johnson, and he faced a major public backlash after the Tet Offensive in January of that year. This assault, which was launched by the Viet Cong and the People's Army of Vietnam, was eventually pushed back, but it took the US forces by surprise and shocked the American public, who were increasingly opposed to the war. Other major events in this year included the assassinations of Martin Luther King (1929-1968) and John F. Kennedy's brother, Robert Kennedy (1925-1968).

The dreams of racial equality in American society and victory for its troops in Asia were left in tatters. Johnson took the decision to limit armed US action in Vietnam and began talks with North Vietnam. After he left office in 1969, he retired to his ranch in Texas, where he died four years later.

ANALYSIS OF THE WAR

A CONFLICT BETWEEN THE SOUTH VIETNAMESE ARMY AND THE VIET CONG (1955-1964)

From 1955 onwards, Ngô Đình Diệm's authoritarian regime introduced a series of reforms with the stated aim of modernising the country. However, no economic reform was introduced, while his new social legislation limited individual freedoms and outlawed all political and public gatherings that opposed the ruling powers.

These new laws only exacerbated public hostility towards Diệm, who openly practised nepotism and introduced policies for the benefit of Vietnam's Catholic minority. A resistance movement gathered strength, and the Viet Minh and Buddhist groups, who were fiercely opposed to his government, aimed to overthrow Diệm and unite the country under a Communist regime.

Initially, the government planned to quell resistance against the regime by eliminating members of the Viet Minh from the territory. To this end, the army waged a constant offensive against suspected Communists and anyone suspected of being in contact with North Vietnam.

The insurgents were assisted by peasant families in the Mekong Delta. From 1958 onwards, their strategy was to weaken Diệm's government by kidnapping or murdering senior officials.

The number of people involved in this rebellion rose from an estimated 2500 at the start of 1959 to 12 000 in 1960. This increase can be explained by the policy of moving peasants in the Makong Delta to the new villages, known as "agrovilles", that were being built at this time. The aim of this policy was to prevent the rebels from receiving support from the peasants and to implement agrarian reform, which ultimately came to nothing.

The government of North Vietnam ordered its soldiers to create a supply route to the region in order to provide military support to the insurgents in the south. This route later developed into the Ho Chi Minh Highway. The first convoys arrived in South Vietnam in August 1959, and from autumn of the same year the South Vietnamese rebels also received supplies by sea. This aid encouraged anti-Diệm insurgents of all stripes to join forces under the banner of the National Liberation Front of South Vietnam.

The National Liberation Front of South Vietnam, better known as the Viet Cong, was created in December 1960 in the city of Tây Ninh. Its members came from every social class and hailed from all over South Vietnam. The movement's leader was Nguyễn Hữu Thọ, a lawyer who had studied under the colonial administration and fought for independence during the First Indochina War. Although the organisation was independent of the Viet Minh, it too fiercely opposed Diệm. Its ranks swelled rapidly, and by 1962 it numbered between 20 000 and 25 000 regular fighters and some 80 000 members.

Starting in 1961, the US president John F. Kennedy provided strategic and logistical support to the South Vietnamese army, which was under attack from the Viet Cong.

US INTERVENTION (1964-1968)

The military coup which deposed Diệm plunged South Vietnam into political instability until Nguyễn Văn Thiệu became president in 1967. The USA was well aware of the problems facing the government in Saigon, and from 1964 onwards undertook military intervention on the ground in order to halt the advance of the North Vietnamese army and the Viet Cong.

The USA initially carried out covert action in order to put pressure on the government in Hanoi. Operation 34A involved armed raids on the North Vietnamese and Laotian borders in order to protect South Vietnam's borders. However, North Vietnam was unfazed by these operations and put up fierce resistance to the US assaults.

On 2 August 1964, commandoes from Operation 34A bombed two islands off the coast of North Vietnam, which retaliated by torpedoing the USS *Maddox*, an American destroyer on a top-secret mission to record North Vietnamese radio and radar signals. As a result of this incident, the USA declared open war on the government in Hanoi, and on 7 August 1964 Congress passed the Gulf of Tonkin Resolution, which authorised the president to use armed force in Southeast Asia.

Operation Rolling Thunder, which involved carrying out bombing campaigns in North Vietnam and sending a further 3500 marines to American bases in South Vietnam, began in 1964. The US military presence in the country increased constantly, from 184 300 soldiers in 1965 to 543 000 in 1969.

| American bomb strike on a Viet Cong base to
the south of Saigon, 1965.

The American military strategy was to wage a war of attrition. The CORDS (Civil Operations and Revolutionary Development Support) programme, which began in 1964 and was intensified in 1967, involved implementing a series of initiatives in the fields of food, medicine, education and material supplies to pacify the South Vietnamese population.

Alongside this humanitarian intervention, soldiers carried out thorough search and sweep operations in South Vietnam to flush out Viet Cong fighters who were assisted and sheltered by peasants. In the most sparsely inhabited zones, namely forest areas, any unidentified Vietnamese were considered enemies to be eliminated.

Viet Cong troops, which were supplied with food and weaponry by the Democratic Republic of Vietnam, China and the USSR, favoured guerrilla warfare. They launched quick surprise attacks before retreating, and spread propaganda among the local inhabitants to recruit new fighters to their cause. Viet Cong fighters hid on underground bases in remote areas, such as the rainforest, which meant that the marines could not drive them out easily. The US troops used helicopters, which were easier to manoeuvre in inhospitable territory, and sprayed highly toxic chemical defoliants over the vegetation in order to uncover and starve the enemy.

| A helicopter sprays defoliant in the Mekong Delta, Vietnam, July 1969.

The use of toxic chemicals had disastrous effects on the environment and on the health of the inhabitants of both North and South Vietnam, and also proved harmful to US soldiers and neighbouring countries like Laos and Cambodia.

In spite of the USA's extensive military manoeuvres, the Viet Cong was still able to surprise the US soldiers with the Tet Offensive on 30 January 1968, in which 80 000 Communist soldiers attacked over 100 towns and cities in South Vietnam. The offensive was centred on Saigon, and the Communists' main targets were:

- the headquarters of the general staff of the Army of the Republic of Vietnam;
- the Independence Palace;
- the US embassy;
- the Long Binh naval base;
- the national radio station.

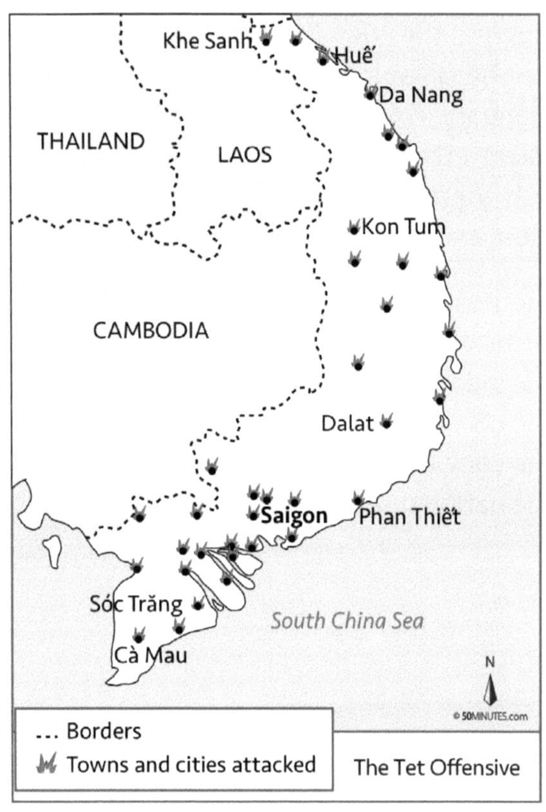

It took the US army 77 days to put down the offensive, and Saigon was liberated in mid-February. The Viet Cong sustained heavy losses and was seriously weakened after the assault, but North Vietnam did not yield, having made a clear statement of its power and opposition to the American armed forces. The American government was left shaken by the attack, especially considering that it already faced vocal opposition to the war from hippies and students, among others, and the decision to draft more American soldiers to South Vietnam was heavily criticised by many American citizens.

DID YOU KNOW?

The Vietnam War received extensive media coverage, in particular from reporters who travelled to Vietnam to observe the conflict at first hand. From its earliest days, it was criticised by intellectuals, then by an increasingly large part of the population, particularly students and the hippie movement.

Contrary to Washington's earlier hopes, there was no quick total victory in sight, so Johnson was forced to alter his strategy. He decided not to stand for another term and unconditionally ended US bombing campaigns in North Vietnam in May 1968. After preliminary talks, peace negotiations officially began in January 1969.

THE GRADUAL WITHDRAWAL OF AMERICAN FORCES (1969-1975)

The Paris peace negotiations began in January 1969 and aimed to put an end to the Vietnam War. The key participants were the USA, South Vietnam, North Vietnam and the Viet Cong, which changed its official name from the National Liberation Front of South Vietnam to the Provisional Revolutionary Government (PRG) in June 1969. The initial phase of the talks aimed to install a new government that would be independent of both US and Communist influence in South Vietnam.

The negotiations failed in December 1972, when American forces began bombing Vietnam again. However, talks soon resumed, and in 1973 a ceasefire was reached and plans were made for American forces to withdraw within two months. The population of South Vietnam was to decide its own fate through free elections organised by the country's three political forces and overseen by multiple foreign countries, including China, the USSR, Great Britain and France.

In January 1973, American troops gradually began withdrawing from South Vietnam. By March, the last American soldiers and the hundreds of American prisoners had returned to the USA. However, in the end the Paris Peace Accords were never fully put into practice, as the South Vietnamese president Nguyên Van Thiêu refused to recognise the PRG and planned to continue fighting North Vietnam, which responded to this provocation with force.

By October 1974, Hanoi officially considered the Paris Peace Accords to be null and void and prepared to take advantage of the weakened state of the South Vietnamese army and the population's war-weariness to embark on a new offensive. Meanwhile, in the face of opposition at home and abroad, the USA was reducing its logistical support to South Vietnam.

In March 1975, the People's Army of Vietnam (the North Vietnamese army) launched a new attack on South Vietnam, and the towns of Quảng Trị, Huế and Da Nang were abandoned almost without a fight. Thiêu was forced to resign on 21 April 1975. North Vietnamese tanks put an end to any attempts at negotiation when they entered Saigon on 30 April 1975, the official end date of the Vietnam War. South Vietnam was then led by the PRG for a transitional period which ended on 2 July 1976, when the two halves of the country were reunited as the Socialist Republic of Vietnam. However, a significant proportion of the inhabitants of South Vietnam fled the new government and went into exile in the USA and Europe.

| South Vietnamese refugees in April 1975.

IMPACT

THE LONG ROAD TO INTERNATIONAL RECOGNITION (1976-2000)

On 2 July 1976, Vietnam was officially reunified and Hanoi proclaimed the establishment of the Socialist Republic of Vietnam, with Tôn Đức Thắng (1888-1980), the former president of North Vietnam, as president and Phạm Văn Đồng (1906-2000) as prime minister. The new nation adopted North Vietnam's constitution.

The new country's economic problems soon became clear, and it was obvious that it would be necessary to relocate many citizens in order to restructure the employment market. This process began in January 1977. The new nation also signed a series of cooperation or aid deals with a range of Western countries, including its former coloniser France.

Political tension mounted between Hanoi and Cambodia, which was controlled by the

Communist group the Khmer Rouge, from 1975 onwards. The Khmer Rouge accused Vietnam of wanting to control it and asked China for assistance to reconquer Vietnamese territory. The territorial disputes between the two countries culminated in a Vietnamese military offensive on 25 December 1978 which toppled the Khmer Rouge and made Vietnam the dominant power in Southeast Asia.

However, the newfound dominance of Vietnam, which had become a Soviet ally in June 1978, left China worried, and it attacked the country on 17 February 1979, marking the beginning of the Sino-Vietnamese War. After fierce fighting, the Chinese troops were forced to withdraw and peace negotiations began. The war continued, but covertly, as China armed Khmer Rouge fighters who remained present in the region until 1991. In spite of this threat, Vietnam's political power only increased. In December 1999, the two countries signed peace and territorial agreements.

From 1991 onwards, Vietnam forged closer relationships with the countries of the ASEAN (Association of South East Asian Nations), and trade and investment increased rapidly. In July 1992, the country signed the ASEAN's Treaty of Amity and Cooperation, and it became the seventh member of the organisation in July 1995.

Vietnam and the USA did not sign an agreement to normalise their economic relations until July 2000, to the great satisfaction of Hanoi, which now saw the possibility of joining the World Trade Organization. In November of the same year, Bill Clinton (born in 1946) became the first American president to visit Vietnam, and in 2002 the USA became the country's primary trade partner, ahead of Japan and China.

TRAUMA FOR VETERANS AND VIETNAMESE CITIZENS

The American soldiers who returned from Vietnam struggled to recover from the psychological shock of their ordeal.

They had had to acclimatise to the tropical conditions in Vietnam, been subjected to surprise attacks which left them permanently on edge, and used alcohol, cigarettes and drugs to pass the time. As it had been drilled into them that the Viet Cong were merciless and unrelenting enemies, they had had no qualms about annihilating them and had turned into killing machines. Captured women were raped or forced into prostitution. The conflict also took its toll on its participants' bodies: some of them were maimed by landmines, while others developed cancer and other illnesses caused by exposure to highly toxic defoliants such as Agent Orange.

All this made it very difficult for American soldiers to reintegrate into society once they returned home. The brutal war was etched into their memories, and many of them struggled to forget the atrocities perpetrated in the name of the policy of containment. Most veterans received some form of psychological treatment, and some were even institutionalised.

The financial cost of the war was high, but the human cost was even higher, with almost 60 000 American soldiers killed during the conflict.

However, the people of South Vietnam were un-doubtedly the greatest victims of the war, with over two million civilians and almost as many soldiers killed. Even children were not spared: between 1961 and 1966, a quarter of a million children were wounded and 10 000 were taken in by orphanages. Millions of children ended up in refugee camps, and many were left homeless.

The effects of the trauma engendered by the war are still felt today. According to studies carried out between 1989 and 1997 on the effects of the war on Vietnamese children, many children between the ages of seven and 13 were suffering from behavioural or psychological disorders such as anxiety, nervous tics and even hysteria linked to their parents' involvement in the conflict.

Like American veterans, the Vietnamese population was also affected by the harmful effects of the defoliants and Agent Orange which were sprayed over the South of the country during the war. Many babies were born with deformities, and cancer became increasingly prevalent. In total, an estimated 4.8 million people suffered harmful effects from these toxic chemicals. Furthermore, while the USA generally granted compensation to affected American soldiers, it took no responsibility for deformations and other traumas among the Vietnamese populations.

SUMMARY

- **26 April-21 July 1954:** the Geneva Accords put an end to the First Indochina War and provisionally divided Vietnam into two separate administrative zones: a Communist-controlled sector to the north of the 17th parallel, and a nationalist, pro-American region to the south.
- **July 1956:** South Vietnam refused to organise the elections stipulated in the Geneva Accords with the aim of reunifying the country. Opposition to the regime intensified.
- **February 1959:** Communists in South Vietnam launched an insurrection against the regime, with the support of North Vietnam and Ho Chi Minh.
- **20 December 1960:** the National Liberation Front of South Vietnam, better known as the Viet Cong, was founded.
- **7 August 1964:** the US Congress passed the Gulf of Tonkin Resolution, which gave President Johnson the authority to send massive numbers of US soldiers to fight in Vietnam.

- **February 1965:** the US army began bombing North Vietnam.
- **January-February 1968:** the Viet Cong launched the Tet Offensive in towns and cities across South Vietnam.
- **31 March 1968:** the USA halted its bombing campaigns in North Vietnam, paving the way for negotiations with Ho Chi Minh.
- **27 April 1973:** the Paris Peace Accords led to US troops withdrawing from Vietnam.
- **30 April 1975:** South Vietnam surrendered unconditionally following the capture of Saigon by Communist troops.
- **2 July 1976:** Vietnam was officially reunified and adopted the name Socialist Republic of Vietnam.

We want to hear from you!
Leave a comment on your online library
and share your favourite books on social media!

FIND OUT MORE

BIBLIOGRAPHY

- Jacobs, S. (2006) *Cold War Mandarin: Ngo Dinh Diem and the Origins of America's War in Vietnam, 1950-1963*. Langham, Maryland: Rowman & Littlefield.

- Journoud, P. (2014) *La guerre du Viêt Nam 1964-1975*. Paris: Éditions Perrin.

- Nguyen, E. (2006) *L'Asie géopolitique, de la colonisation à la conquête du monde*. Paris: Éditions Studyrama.

- Prados, J. (2009) *Vietnam: The History of an Unwinnable War, 1945-1975*. Lawrence, Kansas: University Press of Kansas.

- Portes, J. (1993) *Les Américains et la guerre du Viêt Nam, Questions du XXème siècle*. Brussels: Éditions Complexe.

ADDITIONAL SOURCES

- Bowden, M. (2017) *Huế 1968: A Turning Point of the American War in Vietnam*. New York: Grove Press.

- Galloway, J. L. and Moore, H. G. (2002) *We Were Soldiers Once…And Young: The Battle that Changed the War in Vietnam*. London: Corgi Books.

- Ward, G. C. and Burns, K. (2017) *The Vietnam War: An Intimate History*. New York: Alfred A. Knopf.

FILMS AND DOCUMENTARIES

- *Apocalypse Now*. (1979) [Film]. Francis Ford Coppola. Dir. USA: Omni Zoetrope.

- *Platoon*. (1986) [Film]. Oliver Stone. Dir. USA: Helmdale Film Corporation.

- *Born on the Fourth of July*. (1989) [Film]. Oliver Stone. Dir. USA: Ixtlan.

- *Heaven and Earth*. (1993) [Film]. Oliver Stone. Dir. France/USA: Alcor Films, Canal+, Ixtlan, New Regency Pictures, Regency Enterprises, TAE, Todd-AO Studios, Warner Bros.

- *Vietnam: Secret Negotiations that Ended the War*. (2015) [Documentary]. Daniel Roussel. Dir. France: Al Di Sopro Production.

ICONOGRAPHIC SOURCES

- Ho Chi Minh in 1921. Royalty-free reproduction image.

- Photograph of Ho Chi Minh, taken in around 1946.

Royalty-free reproduction image.

- Ngô Đình Diệm in 1957. Royalty-free reproduction image.

- The self-immolation of Thích Quảng Đức, June 1963. © Malcolm Browne.

- Nguyễn Văn Thiệu in 1967. Royalty-free reproduction image.

- Lyndon B. Johnson in 1969. Royalty-free reproduction image.

- American bomb strike on a Viet Cong base to the south of Saigon, 1965. © UN National Archives and Records Administration.

- A helicopter sprays defoliant in the Mekong Delta, Vietnam, July 1969. © UN National Archives and Records Administration.

- South Vietnamese refugees in April 1975. Royalty-free reproduction image.

IMPROVE YOUR GENERAL KNOWLEDGE

IN A BLINK OF AN EYE !

www.50minutes.com